natura

Ixcatli Ulloa

BookLeaf Publishing
India | USA | UK

Presentation by *BookLeaf Publishing*

Web: www.bookleafpub.com

E-mail: info@bookleafpub.com

ISBN: 9789357215350

First edition 2022

The Grand Instructor

ACKNOWLEDGEMENT

Thank you to the many friends who read through my shoddy first drafts! You guys are AMAZING!!!

PREFACE

"Have you understood the vast expanse of the
earth? Tell me, if you know all of this."

Vachellia Tortilis

Morning arises again over the arid desert -
I watch the sunrise, it's just another day to
endure.
My bark - thorns! I prepare to fend off the
insects that lurk.
I am quite used to now expecting the absolute
worse.
I do have quite the reputation to uphold, you
know.
My ancestors braced the house of the true God
for so long!
Almost 500 years in such service - Yet, even so,
Each day I fight and fight to reject parasites and
wrong,
But it's not in vain, you see, I'm still here -
persistently!
Thickets entangled in the thickets of my closest
friends,
We are enduring together, so I'm never alone,
see!
How I fervently desire to live a life free of end!
So continues the day. Bring on the heat, insects
and drought!
May I always keep my defenses on and friends
around.

Sciurus Carolinensis

So what if I can't be still for long?
What difference would it make?
If I went slower, you'd say "What's wrong?"
And assume your safety's at stake.

What difference would it make
To walk at normal pace on all fours?
Putting my own life at stake
Of getting run over, or worse!

What if I walked at normal pace on all fours --
How would anything get done??
Winter is fast approaching, and worse,
We have begun to lose our sun!

How could anything get done
If I don't learn to live among humans?
We share water, air, sky and sun
So adaptability is our only solution.

I learned to live among humans
And, heck, they don't even notice me.
I'm not an issue that requires a solution.
Unless seen at normal speed.

Because then they notice me
And grow weary of my movements
As if only rabies could cause my speed
Not the fact that I'm probing for nuts.

So why judge bouncy movements
Or that I can't stay still for long?
Whether I look for or hide nuts
You will always find wrong.

Papaver Rhoeas

In a Flanders field I've been known to grow --
And to the one in pain, I am well known --
Hope of relief come when I'm sown.
In a Flanders field I've been known to grow.

After both years of despair, I found you --
We shared a Mediterranean ocean blue.
You dried your tears at the sight were I grew.
After both years of despair, I found you.

Learn to grow after a war so bloody --
Learn to heal after much violent fighting --
Learn to bring beauty to fields so lonely
Learn how to be a Flanders field poppy.

Bison Bison

5

Native blood - we stole your land
And called it our own.
Don't let us forget it's yours.

Hydrangea Macrophylla

You teach us resurrection
When this plant comes back.
I wait for it to happen.

Acoropora Nasuta

I sit in the same place for days. I am not too
proud to admit these are my ways.
 And you feel the need to use me for shelter and
protection and comfort and more. And I sit back
and readily give it all away. I watch you leave
during the day, and at night fall fast asleep
among the safety of the colony. And I don't
mind.

But hark! Who goes there?! A never ending
threat, looking to steal our greatest treasure.
Through territory, war begets. Its ever-wrapping
leaves curl around what we call home, stealing
this place -- our place for sun! Its toxins are
wiping out our greatest families. You aren't
home so I let out a signal that war has begun.
And you, you rush back home. You know this is
your moment, what you've been waiting for!

You came in straight away, tearing at the weeds
like a lion tears on its freshly killed prey. The
toxins that kill us do nothing to you but fill you
with toxic rage. You ingest such toxins at
absolutely no cost, in fact, what is more, it's
actually for your gain!! As you save us, you

find this fighting really protects you. For no creature wishes to ingest a toxic Gibiodon Histrio in this day and age.

And you and your friends finish off the last of the enemy. Once again, we can feel sunlight on our polyps. The colony in unanimous joy merrily waves. And you, belly full, return to your bed where you'll sleep the rest of the day away.

And I keep you sheltered, protected and in comfort and more. Happily, I sit back and let you take it all indeed. For there is no other relationship closer to my heart, than ours, my friend, mutually responding to the other's need.

Coronula Diaderma

I'm nothing but a crustacean
Who met you in their youth.
I was floundering about
And then told to attach to you.

And I haven't left since,
Though at times I've thought about it.
But I can't go anywhere
In you my life is set.

Where else could I find free food?
Where else could I get free rides
To places that bring me nourishment
And allow me to catch glimmers of light?

Yet, at times I pile up --
Any other boat I'd surely slow
With the weight of my anxious worrying --
That's not the case with you though.

Your massive size
Seems to hold me well.
It doesn't seem to bother you,
At least as far as I can tell.

You are my stability.
You're all that is good and all that is righteous.
So, O Great One, Keeper of My Being,
Praised be your undeserved kindness!

Sepia Officinalis

A fish of beauty and wonder and awe,
You hypnotize with your color call.
Charming one that you are
Calling to you prey near and far.

You sneaky one, my dear,
Ruling the reef, inspiring fear
With your camouflageistic gear.
How treacherously you can reappear.

Disguised as gravel and lowly sand,
Disguised as the seaweed that washes onto land,
You stalk your prey as death stalks man
The reef comprehends but the inexperienced
can't understand.

Buoyancy allows you to roam the reef;
A ghostly soul set out to cause grief.
If not seen with own eyes, you'd be a source of
disbelief,
But for years now, your work I've seen.

The harder the challenge, the better for you.
You derive joy from finally breaking through

The solid outer armor of a crustacean in naivety
and youth.
You attract them to your mouth, no need to
pursue.

But hark! What is that shadow overhead?
And why, dear perfidious one, are your eyes
with dread?
The reef triumphantly overjoys, and you
comprehend
If you do not retreat, this is very well your end.

And you do, quickly, with minimal fuss
For you sense the presence of a Tursiops
Truncatus
And she with hunger in her eyes, and vacancy in
her gut --
What better meal that this fish unworthy of
trust?

Every prey has its predator to face,
Yet there are always bigger fish to end a
predator's grace.
Yes, you are quite the charmer in this most
beautiful place,
But beware, dear, even you are at risk of dire
straits.

Deniz

I've read well and heard you compare the sea to
a mere infant,
And I thought what a clever little idea that really
is.
You said it burst from the womb and you
swaddled it as mother.
You raised it for humans, who you're sure would
benefit from this.
You raised it to be beautiful and well-kept,
strong yet graceful.
You taught her how to fix herself up; and when
sick, how to heal.
You set her limits to play in and she readily
obeys.
You taught her how to give gifts and protectively
danger conceal.
She listens to you and houses so much more
you've wisely made.
I don't pretend to comprehend the depth of
wisdom it took,
But I recognize how worthy she makes you of
whole-heart praise.
Oh, Deniz! May I care for her as you would
want to be done,

And please see, as her glory goes to you, the almighty one.

Orcinus Orca

We have more culture than they think, you
know,
Though they give us a bad rep.
They don't realize we're governed by order,
traditions,
In order to determine how to go about next.

My mother taught me
What I will soon teach you, sweet child,
It takes such close knit ancestry
To overcome this chaos of the wild.

But love it, don't defy it,
And when chinook runs low learn to adapt.
Learn how to hold your own,
But lean on your clan even though you are apt.

Take care of your family
But do your best to stay alive.
Don't stop learning these ways
But teach them to be wise.

You will be fine, love!
If I ever leave, you have me here
In these women, this clan, this family.

Value the culture and always have me near.

Trochilidae

I am small and fast and busy — matter of fact, I
know.
I fly up, down, forwards, back, right side up and
upside down
My heart beats twelve hundred times a minute-
stress rules me, yet,
I go 16,000 feet high and 60 miles per hour
Mommy, do hummingbirds get tired from flying
and just want
To swim and float in the water for a while? - Yes
we do!
Sweet child, I love my work and how it provides
for you, see?
Dear, I would love to rest but know that I can
not not-move.
However burnt out, I just have to move along or
else
Winters catch up, flowers don't grow, food
grows scarce and we die
I would love to perch on finger and simply make
you laugh
Yet I wipe my tears, do my work, and continue
to fly.
What's the word, hummingbird?, said to
someone with energy.

But just because I don't stop does not mean that it's easy.

Ciconia Ciconia

It starts by diligent rearing
That turns them into what they become,
It gives them their very title:
The birds of loyal love.

She grows up to an age of maturity
And he admires what she's made of.
They commit to a lifetime of friendship —
The birds of loyal love.

They walk together, talk together
Though a voice there's a lack of,
But they find a way to communicate everyday
—
The Birds of loyal love.

And one day, when the time is right,
A nest is built in the rooftop above.
It's filled with packages of expectancy —
The birds of loyal love.

Never do they lack cover,
For both parent turn to keep 'em gloved.
So children never lack protection —
The birds of loyal love.

Night and day through sun and rain.
Mummy and daddy provide fish, snakes, bugs,
Until two months later the babies practice flying
—

The birds of loyal love.

They don't need mum and dad
So the contractual agreement moot becomes.
Weather eventually changes —
The birds of loyal love.

The birds head for warmer scenes,
Together they live among,
Watching the family grow and thrive —
The birds of loyal love.

Then once winter leaves Selçuk,
The storks return with their beloveds
To the same spot as before to start again.
The birds of loyal love.

Branta Canadensis

I saw some geese yesterday.
I heard their honking --
I briefly smiled to myself.

Danaus Plexippus

Four generations live in me
And I am the the one assigned.
Assigned to return home in traditionality
In order to complete this cycle of time.

They prepped for this day,
They anticipated it to come.
Flying farther and farther away,
They knew some day someone would get it
done.

And here I am,
Strengthened muscles and all,
Ready to fly over lengthy lands
In a body relatively small.

Delicate though I seem,
Please, don't be deceived.
With only 30 percent wingspan on me,
I'll still be found traveling.

This is merely the way
Of my nomadic family.
I return to Mexico forests to complete
The quest of the four generations in me.

Solis

23

Our dwarf sun is the smallest
Yet full of power --
What does that say about you??

Ros

All that is will be all that ever was,
It's not that hard to see.
So why not refresh as the dew does?

Dew is formed merely because
The water that was externally comes to be.
All that is becomes all that ever was.

Evaporation, condensation are caused
Because the roots were refreshed firstly.
Why not refresh as the dew does?

Quiet, gentle and so numerous-
How it refreshes and leaves so quickly.
All that is becomes all that ever was.

So if I'm saturated by your love
Then really, what stops me
From refreshing as the dew does?

For in a world as destructive as a costal flood,
I look toward the future hopefully.
For all that is will be all that ever was.

But in the meantime may I refresh as the dew
does.

Allium Cepa

An onion is like a heart,
Layered and wrapped in a peel,
One that with ease is removed
If you correctly take it apart.

An onion is a body
Cold and tightly wrapped up warm
Living in winter Virginia.
To unlayer? Just make it warm, sunny.

Unlayering coat and scarf
May produce some sweat bullets,
And peeling an onion may
Cause unfeeling eyes to quickly start

So cry over the onion
And cry with the breaking heart.

An onion is like a heart.
It's a root to what will grow.
Place it in water, wait and
See! Eventually, new life will start!

Manus

27

My hands are so small and yet
To you it's enough --
Cut, wrinkled, calloused and all.

Adoptionis

Geese adopt goslings
And monkeys their parentless own.
Why does nature do this?

I heard of a beluga group
Adopting a narwhal.
But does it appreciate it?

Mūsica

Music is art.
Aint it a fact?
Notes and harmonies
Intertwined, merged and stacked.

Music is peace.
Aint it a fact?
People of all colors
Intermingled, merged - just like that!

Music is you.
Aint it a fact?
Your joyous light and dark gloom
Your fidelity and conversely your lack.

Music is me
Aint it a fact?
My anger, my laugh, my mind,
The sound you want back.

But music is freedom —
Freedom from the toxically bad
To be artfully at peace with myself.
And that's the fact.

natura

The home of the stork is in the juniper trees.
The high mountains are for the mountain goats;
The crags are a refuge for the rock badgers.
Yet the extent of this wisdom, no one knows.

Where was I when light began to emit?
Where was I when He created all of it?
So who am I to say left or right
If I didn't invent smell, I didn't design sight?

The home of the blue whale is the sea
The Gibion is housed by the Acropora nasuta
The dew refreshes the tired souls —
Every breathing thing - let it praise Jah!